This book has been published thanks to the kind cooperation of Alejandro Benitez, who made and kept contacts with the Cuban drivers, and thanks to the useful help of Roberto Gatti. I would like to remind my friends and partners Alberto Caniato e Adriano Moretti.

Martino Fagiuoli

First published in May 2001

Printed in April 2001
by EUROLITHO S.p.A.
Cesano Boscone (MI) - Italy

Book design: Studio Pleiadi
Cesena (FC) - Italy
English edition by Marina Beretta
Photolitho: Zangheri G & V, Cesena (FC) - Italy

MARTINO FAGIUOLI
AMERICANDREAMCAR INCUBA

To my sons

MARTINO FAGIUOLI
AMERICANDREAMCAR
INCUBA

CONTENTS

CARS ON THE ROAD

In a country where life seems to have stopped some decades ago there exists a museum which shows its treasures in streets and roads. The marvellous objects it exhibits are the old automobiles from the 1950s, American symbols of wealth and power in those days and now the only means of transport for the inhabitants of this island. Martino Fagiuoli, an Italian photographer in love with Cuba and its people, has fixed them in his photographs before they disappear forever, overwhelmed by the inexorable evolution of times.

Many times, while working in Cuba, I have asked myself what was it that drove me in this direction. It was not the first time I savoured the climatic displeasure of working under a severe damp heat. It was not the first time that I experienced the tension caused by the **well-known lack of organization and punctuality characteristic of the Caribbean people. I was also well aware that there would be all kinds of unexpected troubles. But each single time that I asked myself that question I answered more and more** **convinced that this was "my true work",**

Facing page:

Chevrolet, 1950

Above, from left to right and from top to bottom:

Pontiac, Chieftain 1953

Buick, Super 1951

Chevrolet, 4-door Bel Air Sedan 1957

Chevrolet, Fast black 1949

in Cuba this car is called "Torpedo".

Chevrolet, 4-door 210 Sedan 1955

undoubtedly a different type of work to the sort that I had been doing until not long before. But creativity has never come along with peace of mind and well being, and even less has it come along with monotony. I needed challenges but, above all, I needed to encounter different subjects that would allow me to put my profession to good use. Someone could ask me, why Cuba? Why not a place closer to my house? The answer is always the same, I do not want to get accustomed to an easy life. I need unexpected events, I need mazes, I need to get angry or nervous. It is only then that I conceive the idea, the photograph that is different. It is in these difficult situations that I perceive things otherwise and I am ready to react to the slightest stimulus. But are these real difficulties? The dripping sweat, the

Facing page, from left to right and from top to bottom:

Dodge Sedan, 1957

Chevrolet 52 Panel

Chevrolet 51 4-door Standard Sedan

Buick 57 4-door Special Sedan

This page, from left to right and from top to bottom:

Buick 51 Road Master

Buick 58

Pontiac 56

Chevrolet 52 4-door De Luxe Sedan

lack of a shower, your eyes

Chevrolet 48 Flee Master

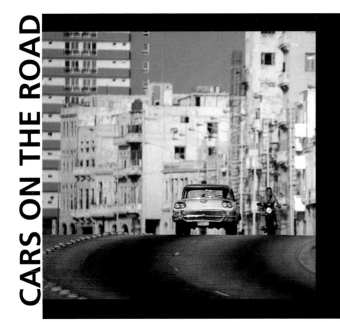

Above, from left to right:

Ford, 1958

Cadillac series Sixty-one, 1950

Chrysler Windsor, 1953

In the middle:

Chrysler Windsor de Luxe, 1955

Facing page, bottom right:

Ford Custoline, 1955

burning because of the light... But this same light is a wonderful light; it changes from one moment to the other, it follows the movements of clouds and breezes. I am in open air, in contact with a changing reality. I live with people who convey me an unexplainable joy of living. Once again why Cuba? Why not Mexico, Jamaica or any other place in Central or South America? For a thousand reasons. For the myths of my youth, Fidel Castro, Che Guevara, Cienfuegos, Hemingway. For its architecture that progresses from colonial to modern, through Art Nouveau and the absurd and rigid Soviet style. For the intelligence, culture, education and dignity of its people. For its unique mix of races, cultures, religions. For its cigars, its rhum, its women... And for the fact that you feel as if **you still were in the 1950s, a period that I have not lived (I was born in 1956), nevertheless a period that has always been present in my family's story, in all sort of literature and films. But what is it that creates this atmosphere? First of all the people, with their rhythm and their joy of living that prevail in spite of**

the difficulties and their countless problems. These people are always ready to stop for a chat, for a laugh, to give you a hand, or to organize a *fiesta* or a *comida*. Then the houses, which have been left unaltered since the 1950s. And most of all the cars, the true symbols of an epoch, the old, noisy and variegated Dodges, Buicks, Fords, Chevrolets and all the others which run fast careless of their age. These same automobiles are the subject of the photographs of thousand of tourists, intoxicated with

the atmosphere they are plunged in. And also I, as a tourist and a photographer, would like to pay homage not only to a marvellous nature, but also to a country and its people, who have succeeded in keeping alive the products of a consumers' society which is not their own, turning them into tourist attractions and creating a huge and unique "driving museum". I would like that my photographs could let you sense

Left, from top to bottom:

Nash rambler American

Oldsmobile Super 88, 1958

Chevrolet 4-door Sedan, 1947

Right, from top to bottom:

Dodge 37 Business Coupe

Ford 52 Mainline

Dodge 57 Coronet

Facing page, left

Chevrolet, 1948

Right, from top to bottom

Chevrolet, 1954

Studebaker Lark, 1960

Chevrolet, 1953

Above, from left to right and from top to bottom:

Ford Custoline, 1953

Chevrolet 59 Impala

Chevrolet 50 2-door Style Line

Facing page, from left to right and from top to bottom:

Plymouth 54

Chrysler 54 New Yorker

Pontiac 51

Ford 52 Grestline Victoria

what difficult reality lies behind these automobiles, but also what is the satisfaction in making them run everyday. In Cuba these cars are the only means of transport. The lack of buses and economic restrictions keep them alive, even when they are just running wrecks. However, in this island of wizards and revolutionaries there are men not so celebrated but as resolute and magic as the former. They are the "family" mechanics, almost legendary figures worshipped by everyone. In my photographic pilgrimage through the country I have seen their "deeds", one could say their "miracles". I have seen how the wiper of a 1956 Buick has been changed for that of a modern Russian Lada, altering the car's original design; I have seen how a tractor's engine, already in the body of an extremely old Chevrolet, has been replaced by that of a big compressor. Such interventions can only be justified in this country, where the cost of labour is minimum and the meaning of time is an extremely relative concept.

Yet Cuba's automobiles are beautiful. They inspire

tenderness. They contribute to an atmosphere of brightness. What I would like to convey to you is the sense of joy these cars

have given me. They have enchanted me, they have made me laugh, and made me angry. I have appreciated how they are

able to create solidarity in people, who participate in the troubles of their neighbours and, when a car needs assistance,

organize veritable treasure troves of spare parts. But no matter what sensations I have felt, I know that I will not be able to

sense them again in the near future. I know that I must seize the moment and enjoy these last years of pleasure and disenchantment.

Things will necessarily change soon and these old

automobiles will disappear, without any fuss, without anyone being aware of this. Other cars, more modern and functional, will take their place, and the old "beauties" will be driven for their last journey. It is for this reason that I have tried to stop them in this book, to freeze their fleeting existence in this peculiar historic period of evolution, so that they will be forever remembered as a milestone in Cuba's society.

Facing page, from left to right:

Buick 53 Special

Pontiac 53

Chevrolet 52

Left, from top to bottom:

Dodge 50

Buick 51

Right, from top to bottom:

Chevrolet Bel Air, 1953

Chevrolet, 1953

VINTAGE CARS

Cars running across Cuba are not only means of transport. They bring back to life the history and glamour of the island, the age of Tropicana nights, of casinos and the revolution. Their design merges with the profile of the buildings, as if the vehicles of the American Dream were part of every aspect of Cuban life. In an age where products are meant to last very few years, these wonderful cars have successfully challenged decades, thanks to the constancy and wit of a whole, proud people.

Martino Fagiuoli, an Italian photographer from Verona with a passionate feeling for the Tropics, has travelled through the city of Havana and areas nearby to capture, by means of his camera, the surviving relics of bygone past which in the western world have been lost forever: a cohort of American automobiles which tell about life styles and social customs of some decades ago. The story which springs from the pages of his traveller's book is the one told by a careful witness, emotionally tied to what he finds in the streets and eager to describe the tiniest detail. Impressions

This and facing page:

Chevrolet 4-door Bel Air Sedan, 1957

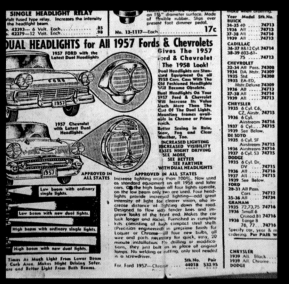

VINTAGE CARS

and notes, subjective sketches and perceptions blend with daily life events, customs and habits, in a direct speech and constant flow with dream. And here it appears a splendid and majestic 1955 Chevrolet, which **takes us back to the old Havana of more than four decades ago, when American automobiles were imported and became a symbol of prestige,** a dynamic component of the city life. One may think this car is an isolate apparition, the fruit of a wealthy collector's fad, whose comfortable economic situation and ingenious ability allow him to **keep running, and in perfect state, that vehicle finished in two tones of blue. The Chevrolet seems as if just purchased from one of those**

This and facing page:

Chevrolet 4-door Bel Air Sedan, 1957

Impressive rear-tailed car; along with the 55-56 series

is the best classic of the American automobiles'

golden era.

It was produced with two engines: a 6-cylinder in line

of 140 HP or a 8V of 283 cubic inches and 220 HP.

3-speed standard or automatic transmission.

2-gear power glide.

137,672 cars of this model were produced.

dealers who sold automobiles in their premises in the high Ambar Motors Building, at the corner of 23 and 0 (in the heart of Rampa Habanera). Or from any other dealer working in the historic and nearby Cayo Hueso, **a district full of shops where, as if pulled out from a magician's hat, accessories covering all possible needs were offered to clients.**

But suddenly, from around the corner, a beautiful aerodynamic Cadillac – the famous "duck's tail" – appears, and we realize that the Chevrolet was not an isolated beauty on the streets of this incredible island. The Cadillac **was once a distinctive symbol for the senators of the Republic, the powerful of the sugarcane industry, for all kind of speculators and, of course, some**

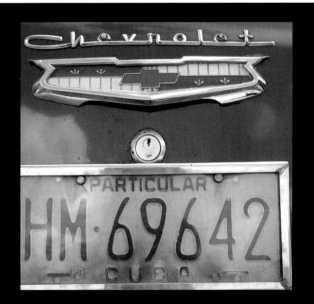

Left:

Chevrolet 55 2-door 210 Sedan

Below, from left to right:

Buick 56 4-door Special Sedan

Pontiac 58 Super Chief

Facing page:

Chevrolet 54 Standard

high-class prostitutes of well known success, whose accidental or semi-regular relations with important men granted them such a life style as to enjoy a luxurious "horizontal property" apartment (Cuban building solutions that favoured the selling of lands and the development of the building industry).

Further away, a Buick is passing by, one with those "teeth" which became more and more protruding, one that radio stations, local newspapers, magazines and the newly-born television advertised by the slogan: "You can have a Buick," illusory assumption that convinced even the most modest worker of the fact that, through monthly payments (the well known "instalments")

he would have the opportunity of driving a beautiful vehicle deemed as the key to absolute and total well-being. But now the tourist's attention is drawn by another jewel which is parading in front of him: a sensational convertible, a huge convertible that smoothly, in spite of its age, runs the beautiful avenue surrounding the famous Malecon

VINTAGE CARS

This, preceding and following pages:

Chevrolet 4-door Bel Air Sedan, 1956

An excellent classic whose great commercial success

took to the production of 1,567,117 cars of all the

models in 1956.

Chromium-plated in all its parts.

It was longer than previous models, more ample

and comfortable; 6 cylinders in line V8,

standard or automatic transmission.

Many cars of the same model were manufactured

even without automation.

and joining, through the extension around the port, the Old Havana to the Vedado; further westward, the avenue links the old town also to the exclusive Miramar district, grown when the wealthy classes moved in that direction and the capital expanded. When in 1959 the revolution won the power, these same classes shifted towards north, beyond the strait of Florida, and reached Miami, a city which, undoubtedly, owes its accelerated development to Cuban immigration. The automobiles (the "engines", the "machines") were left behind, confiscated by the new power, abandoned by their owners to be driven by those who decided to stay in this

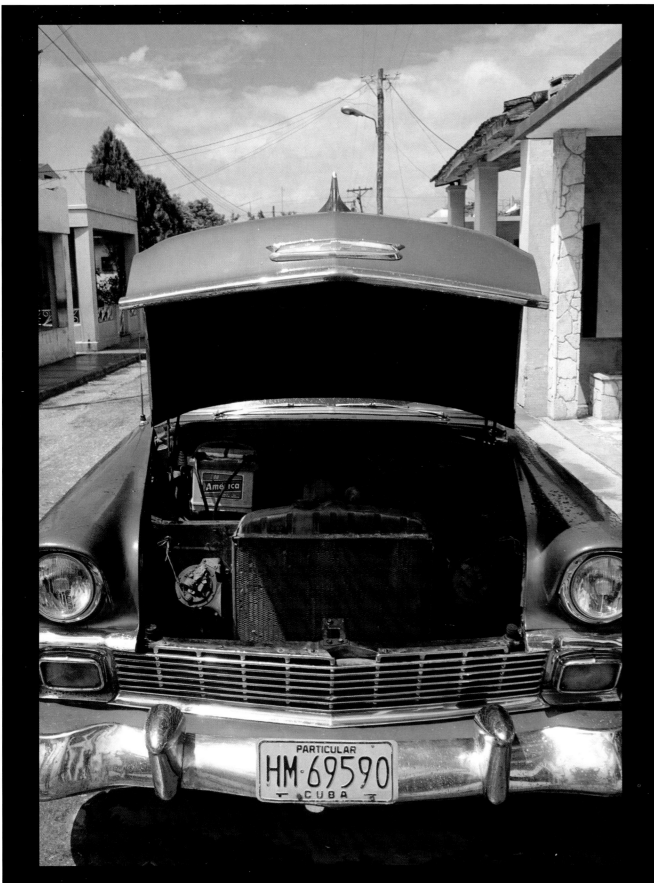

archipelago of which the largest island, the biggest of the Antilles – Cuba – still gives signs of life. In spite of financial restrictions, today the cars made by Ford, Mercury, Pontiac, Plymouth, Chrysler still run. As do the Studebakers whose shape has gained them the nickname of *quimbumbia*, after the game played with a piece of wood, pointed at both ends, and hit with a wooden stick, as if it were a bat from the famous game of baseball.

Mercury 57 2-door Monterrey

Quimbumbia in Cuba was a synonym of enjoyment

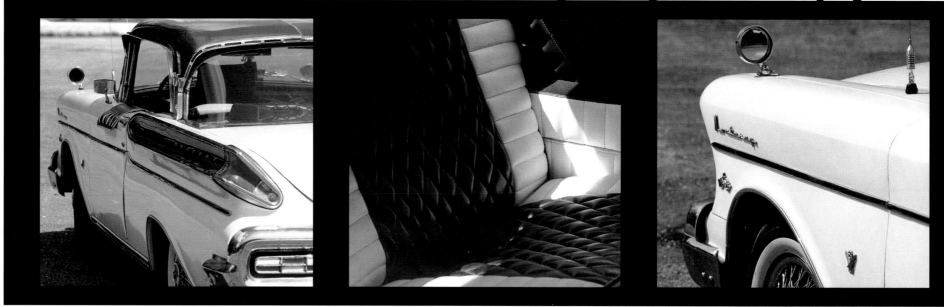

This and facing page:

Mercury 57 2-door Monterrey

A middle-high price range model by Ford with a V8,

312 cubuc inches and 255 HP engine.

Its cost in 1957 in the U.S.A. was of $ 2,693.

42,199 cars of this model were produced.

Huge car with very large interiors, running class

and speed.

Weight 3870 stones.

for so many street children and young people who inhabited the streets of a Havana marked by contrasts. Wonderfully new cars, marvellous middle-class abodes located in exclusive sites on one side; political propaganda spoiling the beautiful avenues with its billboards and slogans, on the other.

This and facing page:

Mercury 57 2-door Monterrey

All this combined with huge brothels, with endless bars which gathered a clientele mainly made up of crews brought ashore by the many ships, and with a swarm of beggars whose poverty harshly contrasted with the brightness of the elaborate neon signs. These were the distinctive elements of the outward face of a country whose public and tourist image was embodied by a world-famous night-club, the *Tropicana* "a paradise under the stars". We are talking of a mask, a surface, a spangle dress that most of times hid both real poverty and the true culture of this melting pot, made of as many cultures and types of blood as we can't imagine. Under the **showy city lay the genuine Havana, a mixture of so many styles and trends, which gave it its own character and personality.**

This and facing page:

Chevrolet 4-door Bel Air Sedan, 1955

In 1955 General Motors introduced major mechanical

and stylistic changes in its Chevrolet division. It was

also the first time that the firm offered, in its low-price

range cars, a new V8 of great displacement, 265 cubic

inches; bore 3.75 inches; stoke 3000 (3.75 x 3.00).

A very powerful engine for that time, featuring

162 HP cdm, 2-core carburettor and 180 HP com.,

4-core carburettor at 4600 r.p.m.

This car is much requested among General Motors' fans

and collectors of vintage cars, because it set an

innovative Chevrolet style which broke with tradition.

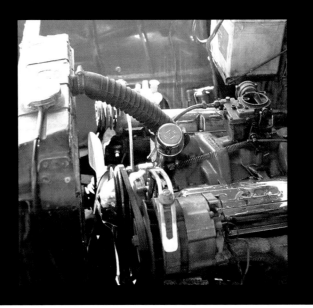

This was the Havana portrayed by the novelist Alejo Carpentier and sung by the poet Nicolas Guillen: "Under the tropical night, the port; / The water laps the innocent shore, / And the lighthouse insults a deserted Malecon." A city that grew up in the sound of drums, that not only favoured the recognizable popular music, but was also the bedrock for the development of cultivated composers, from Amadeo Roldan to Alejandro García Caturla. This was **also the place where the artist Wifredo Lam created**

Preceding page:

Chevrolet Convertible Coupé, 1954

The production of this Convertible Coupé was limited to

19,383 cars. It kept the basic mechanics and body

of the 53 with changes in the front and the rear

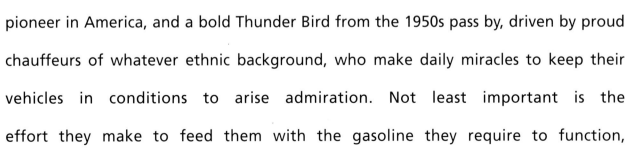

his *Jungle*, a major sculptural work of contemporary art. They all drove those cars that nowadays are an open-air museum, and represent the largest catalogue on wheels ever to be seen. Dates and brands overlap each other: an old Ford from the times in which the industry was

especially in a country where

pioneer in America, and a bold Thunder Bird from the 1950s pass by, driven by proud chauffeurs of whatever ethnic background, who make daily miracles to keep their vehicles in conditions to arise admiration. Not least important is the effort they make to feed them with the gasoline they require to function,

any fuel turns out to be a real luxury, owing to shortages,

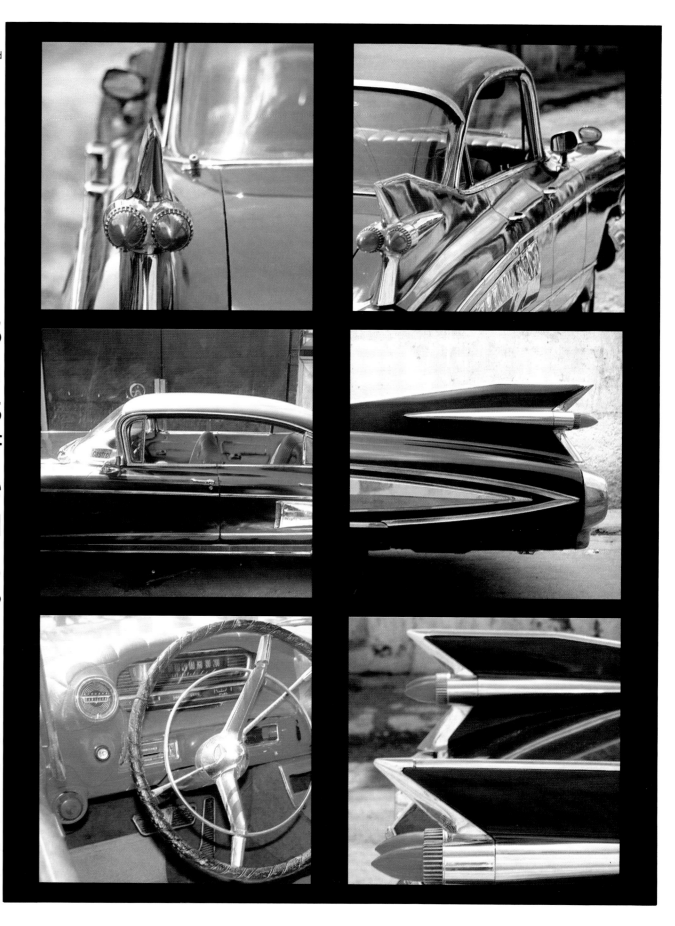

costs and everyday problems of survival which Cuban people must cope with. The cars we see running in the streets of Havana are an integral part of the island's personality, like architecture and other aspects of its culture and traditions. How was it that these cars acquired such a status?

The American luxury automobiles:

General Motors' Lincoln, and Chrysler's Ford and

Imperial, accounting for the 1950s' trilogy of high-price

range cars, symbols of power and opulence.

An enormous and heavy (4890 stones) car.

A V8 engine with 3.90 cubic inches displacement

and 325 HP: 4-speed automatic.

Comfortable car of smooth gears.

VINTAGE CARS

Below:

Cadillac 59 Series C2 Special Fleetwood

Many chromium-plated parts, large rear wings

remindful of space rockets.

Spacious and elegant interior, high quality instrument

panel. One of the largest and most luxurious

American cars of its times.

Excellent classic of which there are only few left.

The answer or even better, the answers, are as varied as vague. Among others, Cuba's geographical position, its prosperity, the necessity and urge of its inhabitants to be up to date; these factors and others resulted in such a mass importation of American automobiles. Moreover there was a market, and automobile dealers saw the opportunity for huge earnings. People wanted cars and did everything to afford them, even when in the family the budget was not enough to buy one. In a way or the other the car reached the family's house, to become part and symbol of a standard of living that required the comfort of a means of transport to cover personal needs, or just the pleasure

of going for a ride all together. The "car" became a status symbol, which gave chances to receive bank loans, get a better job, conquer an attractive partner and make good deals, in accordance with the level in the social ladder the owner reached thanks to his vehicle. Tramways that had once run steadily and regularly along their iron tracks disappeared, and were replaced by buses which polluted the air with their exhaust fumes. The number of cars running the streets multiplied, causing even more traffic jams

VINTAGE CARS

mainly affecting the old heart of the city. The American cars required quite a lot of fuel but petrol could be bought at a reasonable price. The comfort these four-wheeled vehicles offered in exchange was extraordinary, and was matched by a social prestige never reached before. Suggestive colours, magnificent design resulting from the competition between manufacturers, **seduced Cuban customers who dreamt of acquiring a better life style. The short distance between car manufacturers and buyers was**

This and facing page:

Chevrolet 51 4-door Style Line Sedan

Safe and reliable car with simple

mechanics and comfortable lines.

Classic cherished by fans.

Produced as the 1950 model with

2 engines: a 92 HP and a 105

in the 2-speed automatic transmission model.

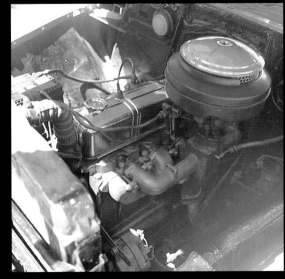

an advantage, given that Havana is only 90 miles from Florida; moreover, the prices were still competitive. No surprise then that these "products of technology" rapidly increased on the streets of Cuba. As already said, quite a lot of automobile owners emigrated,

and went north to drove the U.S. cars. But at least as many did not leave and remained to witness the difficulties in earning a living of the last forty years. They were given the possibility to possess Soviet models, such as Lada and Moskovitch, but some of them did not give their old "jewels" up, and some others received them in the most incredible ways. These men found any kind of expedient to keep such cars alive, and even invented ways to repair bodyworks, retrieve spare parts, make them run for years. It's difficult to grasp how

all this was possible, but the automobiles that continue to run with an efficiency that defies time and space are evidence of such miracle. Getting into one of these cars is like having access to a part of living history, it takes you back to the time in which they were an integral part of a city which, like its vehicles, still possesses the feeling of the 1950s. During those years

This and facing page:

Chevolet 52 2-door Bel Air

It was the first of the famous Chevrolets Bel Air

differing from all the other models of that

same year for its many chrome-plated parts

and rear windscreen.

Much more spacious than others, it marked the

beginning of the era of the sportive coupé style.

A real running jewel, warmly welcomed

by the market.

103,356 cars were produced.

the streets were filled with the products of the American automobile industry, often acquired through established dealers, or frequently brought over directly by the buyers in ferries; in one night those boats could transport a full loading of new and second-hand cars. But how could these icons of the "American dream" survive in

This and facing page:

Chevrolet 52 2-door Bel Air

VINTAGE CARS

This and facing page:

Dodge 56 2-door Custon Royal

A richly decorated model with slender lines, and a grand tourer with a V8 engine of 315 cubic inches and 218 HP. In this car the gear lever placed on the steering shaft was substituted by high-precision selection buttons to the left of the driver. This was the most interesting feature introduced in 1956, an innovation without precedents in the 1950s.

the heart of a society which is expressly

against capitalist policies? The situation in Cuba underwent dramatic changes when it was proclaimed a socialist country. Its economy was then based on exchanges with foreign nations (from all over the world one could say), and technology was basically imported from the United States. All these links came abruptly to an end, and relations were kept only with Soviet countries.

VINTAGE CARS

Left and facing page:

Dodge 56 2-door Custon Royal

Pontiac 56 Chieftain

VINTAGE CARS

Above and facing page:

Pontiac 56 Star Chief Convertible Coupé

The American automobiles, like sugarcane industry, a basic element for the country's economy, were left without spare parts; the consequences of this go without saying. Life was literally paralyzed and what once had been the "dream" turned out to be a nightmare. But such huge difficulties didn't stop these cars from running. Their owners tried to give them a less precarious existence: their engines were changed and wheels were fitted with any tyre available. In short, Cuban people found in their ingenious and optimistic temperament a way **to overcome the frustrations derived from a new quite unbearable situation.**

In the following years the American cars travelled along the path of space and time, until they reached a turning point of their history when the socialist systems ruling eastern European countries disappeared.

Further difficulties arose: changes in financial policies, the need of Cuban industry to adapt to new technologies, a steady increase in tourism which, among other things, brought the taxi service back to life. The state set up its own service, entrusting fleets of old cars to state agencies which often turned the running of a business of this kind to their advantage. At the same time, the owners of the vintage cars – or other people to whom the task was delegated –

This and facing page:

Pontiac 56 Star Chief Convertible Coupé

Excellent convertible of high quality

finishing with electric hood.

A V8 engine of 287 cubic inches and 200 HP

4-speed automatic hydra-matic.

VINTAGE CARS

This page:

Buick 55 Century Convertible Coupé

Facing page:

Buick 56 4-door Special

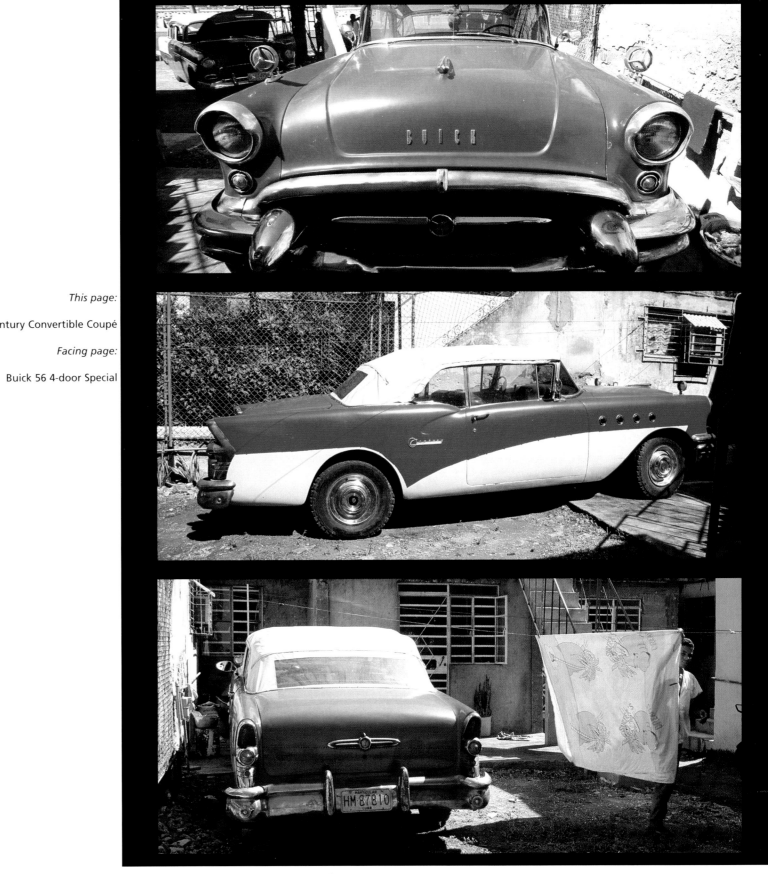

created an unofficial taxi service which grew in size and assured work to the *boteros* (a term used to describe the people who rent their property to individuals or groups). When such activity was legalized, the spacious vehicles were brought back to life and the old pistons, valves and spark plugs resurrected from the past. Who were the people who engaged themselves in such an activity? Mainly out-of-work entrepreneurs, folks with no regular employment and even professionals in need of an extra income, which often exceeded by far their official earnings. They took command of these ancient vehicles which, after necessary alterations, could live their **second childhood or, at least, a lively old age. The return to their past glory was mainly due to substantial restoration interventions carried out**

Previous page:

Buick 56 Special

This page:

Buick 53 4-door Special Sedan

This model was the last of this series.

The old 8 cylinders in line

engines became

part of history; afterwards

they were all V8 engines.

on those vehicles which, miraculously, had been preserved in quite a perfect state by their owners. Nowadays, it's not unusual to **come across a driver who offers his passengers a guided tour of the city, providing historical news,**

pointing out places of interest, best restaurants or dance halls specialized in Cuban *salsa* or *timba*. In short, a vast amount of information imparted clearly and **concisely, and demonstrating how Cuban** people have taken advantage from the many learning opportunities. The "American dream" illustrated by perhaps its most symbolic object is tinged with nostalgia.

This and facing page:

Studebaker 4-door Lark Sedan 1960

Produced with 6 cylinders or V8 engines.

It represents the last attempt of the manufacturer to

revitalize this brand. It disappeared in 1966 due to the

harsh competition of the three giant industries:

General Motors, Ford and Chrysler.

Those who now enjoy a certain economic stability thanks to their commercial activity are not the upper-classes of the past to whom money was no object; neither do they belong to the middle-class, who used their automobiles as part of everyday life. We are talking about a colourful mix of individuals who can be grouped together only in terms of an income obtained thanks to this new and unusual initiative.

This and facing page:

Plymouth 56 Belvedere

V8 engine, 180 HP 2-speed pressure buttons,

automatic transmission.

Large rear wings and decorated dashboard.

Their old cars have taken on new roles, being able of both satisfying tourists' needs and becoming a way to earn a living. The range of uses and functions covered by these vehicles is really amazing. They have been kept by some families only as a memory of past times, meticulously looked after by their owners in an act of love and stubbornness. Alternatively, they have become an instrument to exploit the tourist industry, giving the holidaymakers the opportunity

to enjoy a tour while sitting

inside an authentic museum piece.

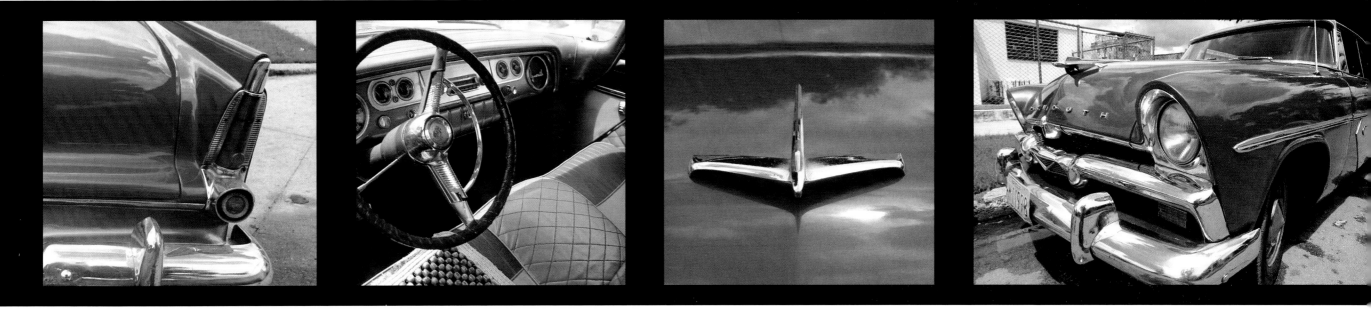

Through their glass windows tourists can make a journey back in time and contemplate palaces – like the Fosca Building, or the edifice financed by the Retiro Medico – whose style dates back to the period in which these automobiles were manufactured. Some other vintage cars are kept by the members of dedicated clubs who like to show them in events organized for their fans. But there is also another category including the vehicles lined up in the area in front of the Capitolio Nacional, where a bizarre cohort of old models – Nash, Packard, Oldsmobile – is parked. They are not so well maintained and not so brightly painted, their engines often cough; they provide a service for local people to go from one part of the city to another, and sometimes even further (intrepid as their passengers and drivers may be!). A little closer to the sea

This and facing page:

Ford 57 4-door Custon Sedan

This model was produced with the already known

V8 and 6 cylinders in line 223 cubic inches on head

valves and 144HP.

VINTAGE CARS

This and facing page:

Oldsmobile Super 88 1960 2-doors

Enormous Grand Tourer, with many glass

and chromium-plated parts.

Colourful and elegant, V8 engine of 394 cubic

inches and 315 HP.

The 1960s models were the last ones to enter Cuba

in the old Casino Español – an excessively ornated building now called Palacio de los Matrimonios, in the centre of Havana's Paseo del Prado – one can have the most curious and timeless experience of his life: a couple arrives intent on formalizing their relationship; he wears trousers, a long sleeved shirt and sports jacket with a tie around his neck. His attire seems somewhat informal if compared to the bride who is wearing a long frilly lace gown with a veil and a long train flowing behind her. She ceremoniously steps out of a magnificent American convertible manufactured forty years ago. It has made its way through the crowd who are cheering the bride thanks to the tune of Wagner's *Wedding March* played by a loud sounding horn.

CAR DRIVERS

The history of vintage cars in Cuba is also that of a few men who came to be united by passion, need and a feeling of brotherhood. From the birth of the Owners' Club to the first, great rally Havana-Veradero-Havana, these legendary vehicles have come back to life thanks to the engagement, ingenuity and inventiveness of the people who take care of them day after day, one generation after the other. This explains the "miracle" of cars in Cuba, and this is the reason why so many tourists and reporters land on the island: to admire this amazing "museum on wheels".

Preceding page, left:

Garage: electrical parts, engines,

starters, alternating dynamos

and wire systems

This page

General mechanical repairs

Antic Ford 24

In 1994 Mr Lorenzo Verdecia,
a producer of the TVC network, needed a few automobiles from the 1930s to film scenes for a television serial; after an arduous search he had the idea to go to the city and look for more of those vehicles that still maintained their original appearance and enjoyed perfect mechanical conditions.

This was the first step that led to the organization of exhibitions of privately owned models from the 1920s and 1950s. The first was held on 30 March 1996. The vehicles gathered in this initial occasion were 50 and the event marked the foundation of a motor club in which the automobiles were divided in three categories: vintage, classic and sport. In the second exhibition held in May that same year **it was possible to gather 112 cars, all of them well kept. Prizes were awarded to autos in the vintage, classic, unique and sport categories.**

Page 104:

Plymouth 54 at the entrance of the paint workshop

The jury was a technical

commission made up of engineers and experts in this field who could boast a sound experience and knowledge of these cars. In February 1997 a major event, the Havana-Varadero-Havana rally, was organized. The race was a plain success followed and enjoyed by thousands of people who gathered along the rally course. It was on this occasion that

Bodywork workshop

This and facing page:

Eugenio, "the wizard of tinplate"

FILIGRANAS DE HOJALATA

Es conocido como 'el mago de la hojalata' y su taller en Santiago de las Vegas es un lugar de peregrinación para todos los dueños de un carro americano de época, que le visitan para que él les fabrique los embellecedores de latón según los moldes originales.

the dates for the meetings of the club were established on every second Saturday of each month, in the holiday resort La Giraldilla. Each meeting has brought the owners closer and closer in a sort of family sharing the love for the maintenance and restoration of these vehicles. Along years they have become linked by something much stronger than a hobby, a feeling which resembles brotherhood. In their meetings, apart from the seminaries on restoration, maintenance, use of lubricants..., they exchange spare parts and they find

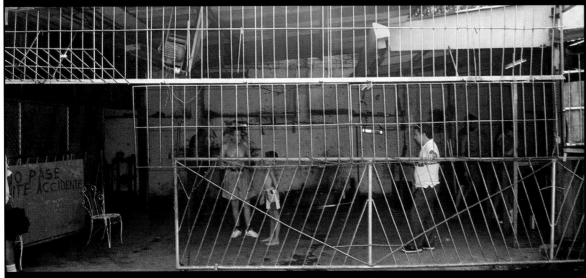

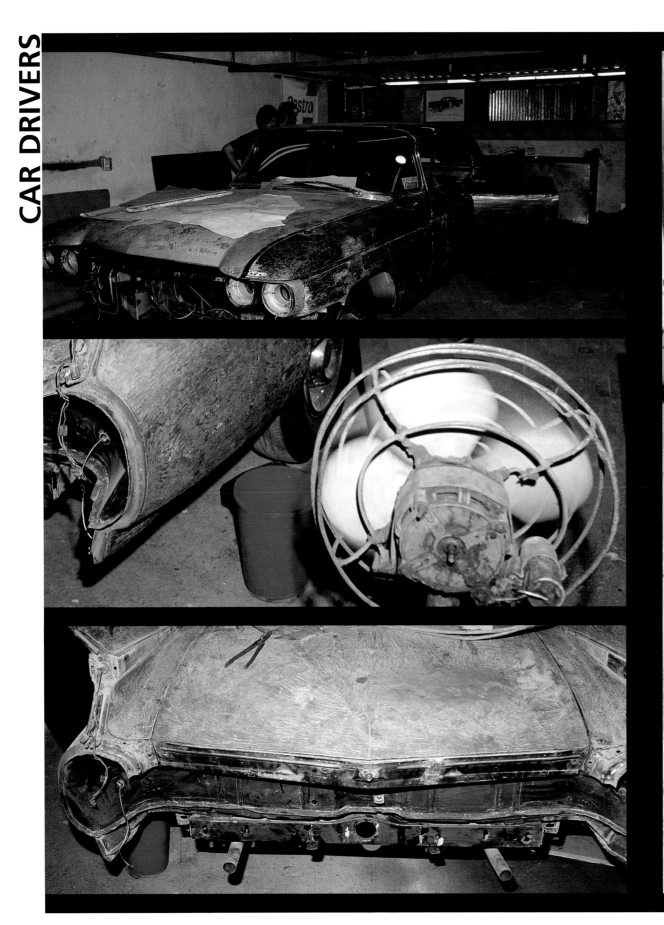

solutions for any member of the club. The association can count on a number of experts in painting, mechanics, tinwork, electricity, etc, who have the difficult task of undertaking all the work using old parts and pieces. These artisans are consequently cosidered like "wizards" who meet the needs of anyone.

This is the case of Eugenio Ohllrams,

a frank, genuine and cheerful person who lives in Santiago de las Vegas where he owns a small garage and where, with rudimental tools, he performs his "magic" manufacturing decorations that help keeping the beauty and originality of old automobiles. In many countries there are collectors who own vintage vehicles, but these are considered "relics" and as such they can only be seen in exhibitions and in parades.

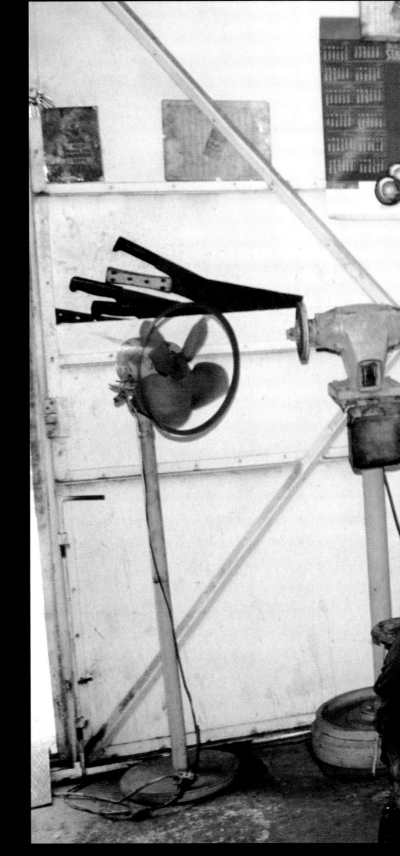

Instead in Cuba anyone has the possibility to admire these old "jewels" in the streets. They have been kept alive by generations of keen persons, and can now still serve their original task as means of transport. This is the reason why in so many occasions the foreign press has told of the "miracle" of Cuban automobiles, and so many reporters and tourists have come to the island to contemplate the beauty of this "museum on wheels". This is the case of the Italian photographer Martino Fagiuoli who, in love with Cuba and its cars, has set himself the task of capturing this incredible reality through his lenses. His work is first of all meant to be a tribute to the tenacity, effort and dedication of those Cubans who have contributed to **the preservation and maintenance of such a running patrimony. Their industriousness and ingenuity, together with Fagiuoli's portraits, give now the opportunity, to those who still have not visited Cuba, to know and appreciate the magnificence of such memories of the past.**

INDEX OF CARS

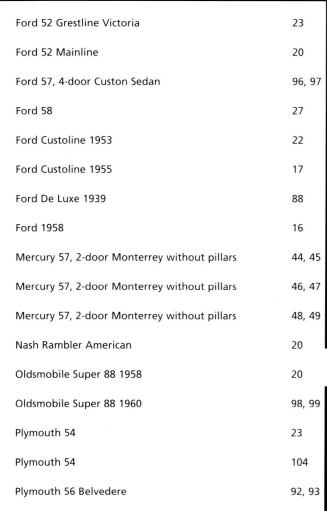

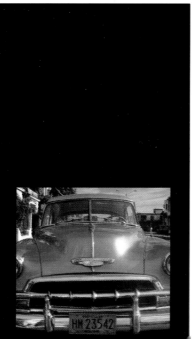